HEIGHTS OF TERROR

Poems by

Patrice K. Owiafe

ISBN: 1-4107-6694-2 (e-book)
ISBN: 1-4107-6693-4 (Paperback)

Library of Congress Control Number: 2003094103

This book is printed on acid free paper.

Printed in the United States of America
Bloomington, IN

1stBooks - rev. 06/27/03

Acknowledgement

I would like to thank Dr. Ian Wight, associate professor, City Planning, University of Manitoba, Winnipeg, for his advice and encouragement.

For the victims of the September eleven, 2001 terrorist attacks in the United States

Table of Contents

Title   page

The number eleven

This was not air rage
Because no hijacker was attacked
And it couldn't be insanity
Because the targets were well thought of.
This was not a coincidence
Because events were well timed
And it couldn't be an act of God
Because the day was godlessly chosen:
The number eleven,
Each figure meant for a tower
Of the beautiful twin towers
Filled with people
That were to be smashed
And ruthlessly brought down
With hijacked planes
Filled with passengers
On this unimaginable day
September the eleventh.

Terrorism

You strike at innocents:
People going to work,
Children hard at play,
Lives filled with love.

You work in secret
Afraid to reveal your face
Knowing how ugly it is.

Lacking the strength for life
And knowing how weak you are
You cunningly choose
The path of destruction
To reduce others
To your own miserable fate.

You choose the path of hate
Because you have no love to give
And the way of death
Because you have no life to provide.

But you must be warned
Yours is a mistaken cause
Because success will not come
By this evil means

And all you'll reap
Is what you sow.

Patrice K. Owiafe

All I feel is rage

As I look at this site
Of destruction and despair
And of pain and horror
All I feel is rage.

As I look at this site
Of mixture of blood and steel
With my eyes in tears,
All I feel is rage.

As I look at this site
Of crumbled towers and spirits
And of destroyed lives and hopes,
All I feel is rage.

And as I look at this carnage
Perpetrated for no other reason
Than a cruel taste for blood,
All I feel is rage.

I remember

I remember September eleventh
And where I was
When the first plane hit
The beautiful north tower
Of the World Trade Center.

I remember this inglorious day
And where I was
When the second plane hit
The wonderful south tower
Of the World Trade Center.

I remember this fateful day
And where I was
When the third plane struck
The south side
Of the sprawling Pentagon.

I remember where I was
When a forth plane dropped
from the sky
And crashed into a field
In Pennsylvania.

I remember the phone calls
From my dear love
Her sweet voice bitter
And her state of shock
Because her heart could not believe
What her eyes were seeing.

I remember I was walking
On Arlington street
Watching cars go by
And wondering whether it was true
That America was under attack
By unarmed civilian planes?

The day after

The sun rains warmth,
Winds lurk on a front
To the east,
Heat rides on a wave
That breaks over our heads,
The sky, clear as the light
From a glowing halogen bulb
Reveals distances
Far across the fields,
Giant mosquitoes—
The attack helicopters—
From the ponds
Take aim at open targets
Laid bare from bikini clad revelers
Sunbathing in the sand,
Sea waves rhythmically
Probe the shore,
Leaves dance themselves lame
To the music of the winds,
Tree branches wave happily
At onlookers
On this delightful summer day
In defiance of the events
Of yesterday
September the eleventh.

I do not believe

I do not believe
The sun did rise
And again did set,
And that winds did blow
And tides did break.

I do not believe
Skies looked clear
And grass looked green,
And rivers did flow
And people did live
On September eleven.

Of gain and loss

This world of sin
Is a place with a face
So ugly and beautiful
It sickens me daily
To relive this life
Of gain and loss.

Is it not insane
To be in a lane
Where all go round
Nonstop to the end
Around a circular crown
Of gain and loss?

Isn't it hollow
To live and follow
This masterful plan
Designed in heaven
To just revolve
Like this moving earth?

Why must I gain youth
Only to lose it with age
And beautiful life
Only to lose it in death?

With this joyful feast
Sure to end in thirst
Sometimes through iniquity
As it did for souls
On September eleven,
I know this life
Is like any day
When we gain and lose
The virgin sun.

If all there can be
Here on earth
Is gain and loss—
A balance without end—
Where is the fruit
Of my daily toils
When unending struggles
Are the feathery wings
With which I fly
This speeding life?

I want to kill bin Laden

I want to kill Osama
For can you believe the trauma
Caused on September the eleventh
By his act of stealth?

What kind of evil thought
Could have led to his murderous acts
On these twin towers
And these other sites?

In my heart I know
Nothing can undo the throe
And the stunning facts
Of his senseless acts.

Yet I'll kill him all the same
For his is a name
That's not fit to be
Where human beings are.

And his is a life
That's not fit to live
For he's a murderous beast
To say the very least.

Patrice K. Owiafe

Who would have thought?

Who would have thought
This normal day like any other
Would be the chosen one
By the destructive forces of evil?

Who would have thought
That an attack of this scale,
Planned in secret
And perpetrated through hijackings
Was ever capable
Of the human mind?

Who would have thought
That innocent passengers
In civilian planes
Could be cruelly flown
To such a dreary fate?

Who would have thought
That humble workers
In polished offices
Could ever be the target
Of such an act of terror?

And who would have thought
That men of religion
Hiding in caves
With unshaven beards
Were ever capable
Of these heinous crimes?

Patrice K. Owiafe

September eleven

Oh terror,
Where is your valor?

Oh furor,
Where is your honor?

Oh horror,
Is this your color?

Or liquor,
Was it your mirror?

Death

Horrid death,
The way you came
On this day
Was so harsh.

Your wry laugh
And what you wrought
With sinister skill
On this city's skyline
Is just impossible
For us to behold.

The places you struck
In such a brazen form
And the ruthlessness
You displayed
In this shameless way
Is just beyond belief.

The thousands you took
So insensitively
And the anguish you caused
With this intolerable plot
Is simply impossible
For us to comprehend.

We heard you

We heard you well
Like thunder after lightening.

We heard the roaring throat
Its stealthy tone,
The menacing shriek,
Your dangerous bark
And deadly cry.

We heard your song
And followed it's rhythm
And got your message
Loud and clear.

And without a doubt
We know what you meant
With your ominous tone
Was a declaration of war
On September eleven.

This dust

Is this dust
Heaped before me
All that remains
Of what was once
A gleaming symbol?

Is this dust
flying about
And coloring the air
Like smoke
The remnants
Of what was once
A scenic tower?

Is this dust
All over my body
And covering my eyes
To the point of blindness
Bits of a building
In which I once worked?

Is this dust
Covering the streets
And rising from the ground

Patrice K. Owiafe

Like vapor
Now the only reminder
Of the World Trade Center?

How could it be?

How could it be
That you who have been
The light that shines,
The star that never pines,
The hand that always caresses,
The heart that never bruises,
And the one who always strives
To brighten every live
Should so glumly
And very brutally
Be carried to your death
By people with dearth
Of honesty and warmth
Taught only to loathe?

Patrice K. Owiafe

Hijacker

Look hijacker,
We thought you were a friend
But now we know you' re not.
We thought you really loved flying
But now we know you don't.

We listened to your plea
And acted with love
Not knowing how insincere
And evil-minded you were.

We gave you a home
Far away from home
But what you gave in return
Was a stab to our back.

Now we have learnt a lesson
Never to be too trusting,
For one for whom you care
May only bring you harm

And one you dearly love
May be the mortal enemy
Ready to give you a kiss
That will bring you death.

UFO

I saw an object
flying north
Opposite the path
Of a shooting star.

I am sure
What I saw
With my teary eyes
Was an UFO
With a silvery cast
Moving silently
Across the sky.

I am confident
That what I saw
Was not a figment
Of my feeble imagination
But a flying saucer
Moving rapidly
Over earth.

Was what I saw
Not from a civilization
High above
Where everlasting peace

Has produced achievement
Far Beyond
That on earth?

Was what I saw
Not from a place
Unlike here
Where our unending rivalries
Make love elusive
Leaving us to live
Daily with terror?

Tears

Tears flowing like a stream
Down a wife's grieving cheeks;
Eyes swollen like a river
Flooded beyond its banks;
Happiness as distant
As the moon
From her shocked life;
All because,
Footloose death
With its incontinent greed
And clothed in terror
Decided to snatch
Her true love
From the very bottom
Of her heart.

A place

Is this a place
Of hope
When it is a place
We wonder, wail
Fail, fall and die?

Is this a place
Of love
When it is a place
We sleep, dream,
Wake and war?

Is this a place
Of envy
When it is a place
We envy
And wish to be
In heaven?

Is this a place
Of promise
When it is a place
Of unfulfilled promises?

HEIGHTS OF TERROR

Is this a place
Of candor
When it is a place
Of addictions
That we are too weak
To abandon?

Is this a place
To dream
When it is a place
Of despair
And madness
Where we wish
Events like those
Of September eleven
Never happen?

Flight 93

You were only passengers
On flight 93
But you showed
Through remarkable heroism
That you were not passengers
But true patriots.

You were flying high
In a hijacked plane
Taking you surely
To death on the ground
But you showed
You were not only willing to die
But ready to give.

They wanted to die
For selfish reasons
For they wanted martyrdom
After death
But you showed your love
In a selfless way
And gave all you could
To save others.

And you showed terror
And its evil masters
That what they plan
Will never succeed
And that those they hate
Are filled with love.

Patrice K. Owiafe

Heights of terror

Could we have known
The heights of terror
If we had not seen
Terror set ablaze
The attractive towers
Of the World Trade Center?

Could we have known
The heights of terror
If we had not witnessed
The heartlessness
With which it put to death
Three thousand
Innocent lives?

Could we have known
The heights of terror
If we had not beheld
A hijacked plane
Tear through
The south tower
Of the twin towers
Leaving behind
This fire and dust?

How long?

Oh Terror
You should have been the one
To depart earth
On September eleven
But it is hard to believe
That you live
And you were the one
Who caused the death
Of these thousands
Of promising lives.

Is it not a curse
For you to remain in our midst
And strike hard blows
On our soft hearts?

And are you not trash
If all you do is thrash
Clean and hopeful
And beautiful lives?

This beauty of our love

This tragic end
To your innocent lives
Is one thing
I'll never understand
But I know
That though you suffered
So much
You do not envy
Us who are alive
Because though you left
In a dreadful way
You live
And experienced this life
That we live.
For though our days
May outnumber yours,
You saw the sun
That we see
And felt the winds
That we feel;
You saw the stars
That we see
And the sun
That we see;
You saw the trees

That we see
And watched the birds
That we watch.
There is nothing we have
That you never had.
And though you suffered
Unfeeling terror
With your bodies,
It also brought
Equal pain
To our hearts.
You also know
That our love for you
Is as much
As you have for us
And that the only loss
To us all
Is that
We can no more
Have the hugs
And kisses
And together enjoy
This beauty
Of our love.

Fire

You burn red hot
And shoot
Massive waves
Of fiery flames
In to the sky.

Your heat can be felt
From afar
Because your magic
Contains a message of hope
And has a glowing
And distant reach.

You give the light
That helps us see
In the dark
And the heat
For the smelter
That produces structures
That when we see
Lift our spirits
And warm our hearts.

HEIGHTS OF TERROR

You sweep through
Fields that keep
Our wildlife
From encroachment
And tear down
The walls that house
The pain of our toils.

But this morning
You brought death
And left
Bruised and burnt hands
And dark marks
On the faces
Of our firefighters
When they only came
To the twin towers
To ensure
That your fiery flames
Do not leave despair
Or consume the hope
Instilled in our hearts
By your warmth.

And your towering flames
Reduced the towers
To a shower of dust
That contains the bodies

Of our dear ones
Who came here
Dressed in love
To fulfill
Their commitments
To the loved ones
They left behind.

But we know
You are a force
For good
But was only used
By evil men
To reduce beauty
To this dust
That now clouds
The sky,
Our future
And our hopes.

A wish for a mother

Mother of all terror
I hope
This abominable birth
That produced
This notorious child
On Nine Eleven
Shall be your last.

May you never receive
Honor
As a mother
And may this diseased
And ugly
Child of yours
Remain totally insane.

And may its hopeless
And brutish life
Be very hapless
And miserably short
And barren.

Patrice K. Owiafe

A terrorist strike

This is not Tyson's bite
Or Harding's strike
And it is not hurricane Andrew
Or a Texas flood.

This is not a piece of Pearl Harbor
Or a portion of Hiroshima,
This is a fiery battleground
In the center of New York.

This is not a volcano's wrath
Or an earthquake's ruin,
It is a misguided strike
At the heart of a nation.

This is not the hand of religion
Or an answer to prayer,
It is the face of terror
After its journey of rape.

The wind that blew

What type of wind
Did mercilessly blow
Over this tranquil place
On September eleven?

What type of heat
Did move this wind
And what type of pressure
Did produce its force?

What type of mind
Did plan its course
And what type of hand
Did steer its flow?

Why did heaven permit
Such an evil wind
To blow freely
Without being blocked?

Why didn't natures cures
Reduce it to a gentle breeze,
Allowing it to cause
This irreparable harm?

Patrice K. Owiafe

A place to visit?

Though this is hallowed ground,
Are these toppled towers
Lying crumbled to the ground
A place to visit?

Is this a mountain peak,
A camping ground,
A boating site,
Or a hunting place?

Is this a sandy beach,
The Golden Gate,
The Empire State,
The Great Wall,
Or a colorful cliff?

Is this not a depressing site
Of the triumph of evil
With images of horror
That are impossible to behold?

Is this not a virulent cauldron,
The site of a crime,
A postmark of terror,
That needs to be shunned?

For with these visitors,
Won't terror feel
It was a religion
Capable of attracting
Pilgrims to its sites?

Our journey

As we look back
On our lives
We can see
How far we've come
On this journey
And yet
As we look forward
We still see
How far
We have to go.
We have overcome
Numerous dangers
And hoped for an end
To all our throes
But God
You know you left
The wily serpent
In our midst
When he should forever
Have been banished
Given the severity
Of his lies
And the unbelievable evil
That he brought
To mar the beauty

Of the Garden of Eden
Making us forfeit
Our life in paradise.
But we know
It is your love
That set him free
For you know
That out of evil
Can come good
And good is so powerful
It can defeat
Any harm
Wrought by evil
And today
September the eleventh
The evil serpent
Did strike again
Through stealth
And lies
To remind us
That he is still in our midst.
But we are not shaken
By this evil act
Because we trust
Your power and judgement
And we know
That out of this evil
Shall arise

Even greater good
Because the devil's power
Is a sham
For it is always afraid
And acts in secret
Because it knows
It will suffer only defeat
Should it ever come out
Into the open
Or wherever it dares show
Its ugly head.

This is not the way to go

This is not the way to go
In the middle of our grief
For our lives must still be lived
Despite the misfortune we've had.

This is not the time to cry
Despite hearts that are broken
For every life is still a life
That must be lived to the full.

This is not a time to lie
Afraid to get up and act
Though all the nerves in our hearts
Have been torn apart by pain.

This is not the way to go
Because things will only get worse
From this point where they are
If we do not face life with strength.

Oh terror!

Oh terror,
Where is
Your restraint,
Your beauty,
Your love?

Where is
Your conscience,
Your insight,
Your heart?

Where is
Your modesty,
Your sincerity,
Your morality?

And where is
Your mind,
Your guilt,
Your shame?

Venomous terror

Venomous terror,
You were determined to choke
The free lifestyle
With deadly toxin
After hauling thousands to death
Through malicious strikes.

When you are so hollow
In thought and spirit,
Why did you think
You could succeed
When you lack the fundamentals
Required for success,
Which are a noble cause
With respect for life?

And why did you think
You could succeed
When your evil light
Cannot illuminate
But only gives
This gruesome chill?

What will freedom serve?

Of what use is freedom
If its own goodness
Becomes its weakness
To be exploited by those
Who want it destroyed?

What will freedom serve
If it should fall asleep
Only to be struck and weakened
Or probably never wake again
From evil acts
Of insidious terror?

With this scale of destruction
In the center of a city
What other proof
Is needed to confirm
That the enemy has the desire
But lacks the means
To flatten every structure
Of this land?

And what other sign
Is needed to reveal
That freedom's enemies

Are ready to set ablaze
These unrivaled values
That make us free?

Patrice K. Owiafe

I won't be overcome

Though it looks like any day
Today is like no other day
Because of the misfortune I've had.
And the loss I have suffered

This day is hard to bear
For it is like being struck with a spear
And the resulting open wound
An impossibility to behold.

It is not easy to understand
How a day can make a difference
And bring a change to my life
That's so difficult to accept.

But I won't be overcome
By this disaster in my life
And will not weakly succumb
To this anguish that I feel.

For this change in my life
Though difficult to bear
Brings only a chance
To make adjustments to my life.

The costly price

As this is a place
With such a desire for peace
Can we only rant
But not get what we want?

Is the costly price
Of this painful lack of peace
Not just too much
For things to remain as such?

Since we know what it takes
To honestly rout the stakes
Why can't we this effort make
Because of what's at stake?

For if we truly want
And fight without relent
Can't we peace attain
When there's so much to gain?

Or do we talk of peace
Only for ourselves to please
When we often appease
Those without a desire for peace?

Patrice K. Owiafe

Giving

Why do we loath to give
What we all yearn to receive?
Though there is a lot we lack
There is something we have
That's very good to share.

Why is it so hard to give
What each one needs to receive?
And when we give, why so little
When there is a lot to receive
For everything we give?

When we are given so abundantly,
Why do we give only sparingly
This great gift of love
And thereby deny to one another
A free gift of life?

The highway

You are wide and winding,
On your sides are trees
That swing with the wind
And at your center
A pale yellow line
That shows
The divisions of life.

You have been here
For decades
And have experienced
What we experience:
The harshness of life
With its extremes
Of heat and cold.

You go distances
Long and short
Passing through
Fields and hills
And wind your way
Delightedly through
Towns and cities.

You are the one
That we cross to meet
The love of our hearts
And the way we take
To cure our plight
Of homesickness.

We are glad you have
Steel bridges that hold firm
And help us cross
Rivers, large or small
With our loads.

When we step on you
We do
With confidence
Because we know
You always lead
To a destination
And never to nowhere.

We do not know
How our lives
Would have been
Without your unbending will
That's in place
To respond to our needs
As we carve out

HEIGHTS OF TERROR

Our individual paths
That empty
Into this river of life.

When we step on you
To lead our lives
We know you will not fail
To lead us where you go
Which is where we want.

You are the very one
Who opens the opportunities
That we enjoy.
You are the hand that guides
Our feet,
The light that leads
Through the darkness,
And the truth that helps us
Stay on course.

You are the long page
On which our short histories
Of here and there
Are proudly
And hastily written
And your history

Is the book
That tells the story
Of our lives.

But today,
September eleven,
You have been covered
By debris
From the twin towers
Leaving us stranded
And without a clue
As to where to direct
Our steps
And lives.

While the shower
Of dust
From this fallen landmark
Of history
Clouds our future
And blinds us
Making it impossible
For us
To see and define
And know
Where to direct
Our lives and hopes.

Let's roll

Let's roll
Because their evil plan
Is to take us and many more
To death on the ground.

Let's just roll
For we must return the love
Others selflessly gave
So we may live.

Let's not recoil
For this is our chance
To lay down our lives
For those we love.

For us death is certain
But for others it is not
So let's play our part
So they may live.

Let's respond to this call
For as patriots
We can't afford to fail
When duty summons.

The task may be grim
But all we need is gallantry
So let's roll
No matter the toll.

For the hour has come
To bring this plane down
And show those we love
That we'll never let them down.

What do I call this act?

What do I call an act
Defying all description
Perpetrated so wickedly
On September eleven?

Do I call it an act of madness
Or one of cowardice?

Do I call this brute cruelty
Or just sick inhumanity?

And do I call it blind hatred
Or a heartless thirst for blood?

I will always be at a loss
As to how to accurately describe
This unspeakable act of murder
Committed on September eleven.

Patrice K. Owiafe

A memorial?

This hole in the heart
Of New York city
Is a sickening sight
That needs to be healed.

This hole must not be left
Only as a memorial
And be made a testament
That death has a place
Deep in the heart.

This hole must be filled,
The tissues must be restored,
What was lost must be regained
For the heart must beat again
And the enemy must feel the pulse.

For we must remember
The plan of the enemy
For sacred ground zero
Was to make it a site of death
And a memorial for the dead.

Why look back?

Why look back
On what you've lost
When all that may be left
Is a heart that's broken?

Why ever look back
On the chances you've missed
When all you may see
Is a heart filled with regret?

Why even look back
On the pain you've had
When all that may remain
Is a soul filled with sorrow?

And why ever fall back
On the tears you wipe
When they are enough
To sweep you away
And have you drowned?

Patrice K. Owiafe

This picture

Is this bright picture
Of fallen Towers
Hanging on this wall
Not the cruelest thing
One could ever see?

Does this vibrant image
Of evil
Just not revive
Painful memories
And relive
Terrible moments?

Is this black and white
Image
Really not another weapon
Pointed at me
By design
By the insatiable masters
Of this act of terror?

And is this image
Hanging on this wall
Not only fit to be

HEIGHTS OF TERROR

In a cave of darkness
Admired and directed
Only by the devil?

Patrice K. Owiafe

The flag

This torn
Star-spangled banner
Flapping like the wings
Of a colorful bird
Was cruelly attacked
On September eleven
With the hope
That a massive blow
From hijacked planes
Hitting buildings
At high speeds
Will tear it apart
And send it flying
Disgracefully to the ground
But these steely colors
Of valor and candor
Refused to fall
For the stars
Show how distant
One has to go
And the red lines,
The powerful defenses
That must be weakened
Before its will
Can be broken.

I am filled with pride
And I am glad to see
That though torn apart
This faithful banner
Retains its color
Of purity and innocence
As it proudly waves
With vigilance and perseverance
At those gathered here
In remembrance of the hour
Its enemies pitifully hoped
That a strike at this site
Where once stood
Two of the world's
Tallest buildings
Will leave it shredded
With its will broken
And its pieces mixed
With the ruble and body parts
That were sent flying
With sorrow and horror
On this sacred ground
On that dreadful day,
September the eleventh.

Patrice K. Owiafe

Is it true?

Is it true
That this hole
Of destruction and death
In the center of New York
Was caused
By an act of terror?

Is it true
That a sight
So distressing to see
At a place
Once filled with life
Was caused
By an act of terror?

Is it true
That this cloud
Escaping from the ground
Like darkness
At the approach of dawn
Was created
By an act of terror?

HEIGHTS OF TERROR

Is it true
That this destructive mess
Billowing fire
So visible to all
was produced
By an act of terror?

Is it true
That the twin towers
That rose to the skies
In such an imposing
And brilliant form
Were brought down
By an act of terror?

And is it true
That lowly terror
Anchored by the devil
Did really reach
These very staggering
And appalling heights?

Patrice K. Owiafe

You went to work

The labor of the righteous
Contributes to life
So you went to work
In the North Tower
Of the World Trade Center
Early this morning
To feed your family
Arriving just before
The first plane hit
The very building
In which you work.

I tried to reach you
But I could not
When news broke
That your place of work
Where you labor
With all your might
Was under attack
And that the very floor
Where you work
Was the very floor
That the first plane struck
Early this morning.

HEIGHTS OF TERROR

I went to the hospitals
And all the makeshift places
Treating the wounded
But I couldn't find you.
I held your photograph
High for all to see
And asked all I met
If anyone had seen you
But I never got an answer.

Now it is late
In the evening
At the time
You are usually home
But you haven't arrived
And you haven't called.

And now all
That's left for me
Is to wait
And cry and hope
That by some miraculous hand
You managed to escape
This appalling disaster
And gained delivery
From the wickedness
Unleashed today

Patrice K. Owiafe

By the forces of darkness
And my worst fears
Will never be confirmed.

Anthrax

Where from this anthrax
That has fallen like an axe
To add to the pain
Of September eleven?

Where from these spores
That are making life sore
With all looking frail
Yet not leaving a trail?

Where from this scourge
That has come to gorge
Our hearts with the fear
That Armageddon is near?

Patrice K. Owiafe

This load

Does this truck load
Of debris
Being hauled
From this site
Of destruction and death
Contain a fragment
Of the sacred remains
Of my missing loved one?

Does this mixture
Of earth and steel
And flesh and blood
From the collapsed towers
Of the World Trade Center
Contain unidentifiable
Sacred fragments
Of my missing loved one?

Does this load
Of debris
Which was once
What that stood
And all that lived
As the World Trade Center

Contain fragments
Of the sacred remains
Of my missing loved one?

Patrice K. Owiafe

Is there someone higher?

Is there someone higher
With great providential power
Who in his two hands holds
Everything that unfolds?

Is he so knowledgeable
He made life so malleable
To withstand fire and flood
And thunder and cold?

But with all the power
Why is so much terror
Permitted to rain
And cause us this pain?

Responsibility

We know you abhor
All that's before
That revels in sameness
Without regard for fairness
For when you created the world
You simultaneously unfurled
Your bounteous love
With unimpeded resolve
Because you know
That for life to flow
With great beauty
And with things in plenty
This must be a place
With a trace
Of colors and flavors
And winds and seasons
And everything that fills
The heart with happiness.

So when we see the rainbow
We immediately know
It is because you are
What you are
A lover of variety
And again of unity

73

For how can life be whole
Without an endless pool
Of tastes and paths
And faces and lives
That may look strange
Yet must bring the change
When winds get strong
Or things go wrong?

And we know
This intermittent flow
Is because you are
What you are:
A responsible being
Who is all knowing
And who created us
Because you wanted us
To be responsible
In all we're capable
And if things slow
Or sometimes don't flow
It isn't because
You run this course
As an unfeeling monster
And a great benefactor
But it is because
In our every recourse
You want us to celebrate difference

Not with vehemence
But with acceptance
And true reverence
In every humble
And courageous way possible
So that our narrow judgements
May not encourage the myths
That breed enmity
Or fuel the fires
Of our deviant desires.

Patrice K. Owiafe

We cry hourly

We cry hourly
Because of this terror
But is this the only time
We have suffered pain?

Our sobbing never ends
Because things are unbearable,
But is this the only time
We've had a heavy load to bear?

We have fallen weakly to our knees
Because of this disaster
But is this the only hour
There ever has been mischance?

Is the anguish we feel
Rather not a daily reminder
That we must be strong on our feet
So we can outflank this evil?

Change of heart

Some have argued that
Of what use is punishment
If it makes the living lament
And leaves the dead in peace
Though the ax is fierce?

For, if punishment is in a form
That it cannot reform
And its purpose is to avenge
Then is it not only revenge?

And what type of punishment
Gives the same suffering
To the guilty offender
As the innocent sufferer?

Others have argued that
Is one raped
If one rapes
And unpityingly ripped
If one rips?

And if death is punishment
Then who is free
From a universal chastisement
To which we'll all be subjected?

But after witnessing this terror
Of September eleven
Shouldn't their faith be weakened,
Giving them a change of heart?

If justice is to be served
Don't it's perpetrators earnestly
deserve
Nothing more and nothing less
Than what they themselves
unleashed?

And since these acts of terror
Were acts of evil
Meant to bring death
To innocent victims,
What other sentence
Perfectly fits this crime
Than one that puts to death
The very guilty beings
Who cruelly planned
These depraved acts of terror?

A day

If there ever was
A day of unexpected loss
In the history of a nation
Then it must be September eleven
The day that produced
A hundred thousand truckloads
Of debris at the site
Of the World Trade center.

If there ever was
A day of unbelievable shock
In the life of a nation
In time of peace
Then it must be September eleven
The day that left
Three thousand dead
And several thousand tons
Of debris at this site
Of mindless, merciless killing.

If there ever was
A morning of untold tragedy
In the life of a nation
That was not at war
Then it must be September eleven

Patrice K. Owiafe

This day of unspeakable terror
When the World Trade Center
Was eerily reduced
To an unbelievable heap of rubble.

We'll never forget

We'll never forget
What terror did
To New York city
And to our loved ones
On September eleven.

We'll never forget
The sight of a plane
Crashing through a tower
Of the World Trade Center
On September eleven.

We'll never forget
The bombing at the State Department
And the crashing of a plane
Into the Pentagon
On September eleven.

We'll never forget
That hallowed spot
Near Shanksville
Where a plane went down
In a peaceful field
On September eleven.

And we'll never forget
The thousands we lost
The shock we felt
And the blow to our psyche
On September eleven.

How can terror win?

How can terror win,
When all it brings is mayhem?

How can terror win,
When all it projects is depravity?

How can terror win,
When what it promotes is inhumanity?

How can terror win,
When all it encourages is chaos?

And how can we enjoy victory,
If force does not stay the course?

Patrice K. Owiafe

Why is life so frail?

Why is life so frail
That it can suddenly fail
On this envious trail
That the heavens hail?

Why do we mourn
When before it's morn
Someone will moan
As a heart is torn?

Why this despicable gloom
Where life always blooms
And why must evil loom
And have such sumptuous room?

Why do we fawn
When before it's dawn
Night would be worn
And love would be drawn?

And why should so much hate
Be part of our fate
When this is a state
Where we all relate?

Could we have imagined?

Even if we were not distracted
And were very attentive,
Could we have imagined
Such a day of terror?

Even if we were awake
And never for a moment misjudged
The nature of terror,
Could we have imagined
Such a day of terror?

Even if we were alert
To the sordid furtiveness
Of acts of terror,
Could we have imagined
This day of terror?

And even if we were insecure
And were not feeling complacent
And did not well forget
That terror was ever present
In our hate-filled world,
Could we have imagined
This a day of terror?

Patrice K. Owiafe

Why?

Why is this a place
Where games end in defeat
And life in death?

Why is it a place
Where we must be ready and alert
And always imagine the worst?

Why is it a place
With so many sides
On which we always have to fall?

Why does it have
Men with evil minds
Always willing to harm
People of good intent?

And why is it a place
Of people with terrorist plans
Ready to bring to ruin
All we strive to build?

Looking forward

Its time to look forward
To the life ahead
And forget the past
And all the bitterness
That this tragedy has brought.

Its time to change course
And set our hearts on a new footing
And forget the loss
Despite the struggle we waged
In expectation of better results.

Its time to accept this fate
And know it can't be changed
For all we lost today
Is all we can have
Which grief cannot change.

And its time to be on our feet
And do all we can
So the mistakes of the past
That produced this tragedy
Are never repeated again.

About the Author

Patrice K. Owiafe was born in Ghana. He studied at the University of Ghana and the University of Oslo in Norway. In 1997 he came to Canada to pursue a master's degree at the University of Manitoba. After completing his studies, he became a Canadian citizen and is now living in Winnipeg. He is the author of the inspirational poetry collection entitled *Tides of Life*.

Printed in the United States
1238100001B/271-294